None
Dare Call It Reason

None
Dare Call It Reason
How the Average American has Hanged Himself

Richard Sutherland

iUniverse, Inc.
New York Bloomington Shanghai

None Dare Call It Reason
How the Average American has Hanged Himself

iUniverse books may be ordered through booksellers or by contacting:

iUniverse
1663 Liberty Drive
Bloomington, IN 47403
www.iuniverse.com
1-800-Authors (1-800-288-4677)

Because of the dynamic nature of the Internet, any Web addresses or links contained in this book may have changed since publication and may no longer be valid.

ISBN: 978-0-595-41028-6 (pbk)

ISBN: 978-0-595-85382-3 (ebk)

Printed in the United States of America

Contents

Introductory Biography

Richard Rogers Sutherland is a 6th generation Texan, descended from ancestors who fought in the Texas War of Independence. Two great, great grandfathers, one great grandfather and one uncle fought in that war. His great-great-great uncle, William Depriest Sutherland, son of his great, great grandfather, George Sutherland, died fighting at the Alamo. Richard is descended from the Adamses of Massachusetts on his mother's side.

Richard discharged his military obligation to the nation by spending four years in the U.S. Army as an intelligence analyst/interpreter/translator in Chinese Mandarin during the 1960's. Following his honorable discharge from active service, Richard resumed his education, earning a B.A. degree in political science/history from Whittier College in 1965. Richard then earned graduate degrees from USC and Harvard in history and Far Eastern Languages before obtaining a J.D. degree from Harvard Law School in 1973. Richard is now retired from litigation law and lives with his wife and two daughters in California.

Section I:
Average Americans have doomed themselves financially.

Let's not beat around the bush. We, as American citizens, are in terrible shape financially. There is no guarantee that your pension plan, if you have one, will be in place when you retire. Chances are at age 60 or 65 you'll still be waist deep in debt, spending much of what you make paying interest on a home mortgage, a car loan or a credit card. Social Security and Medicare are now on wobbly legs. Starting with the "Reagan Revolution" in 1981, we've allowed our national debt to increase more than nine fold in just twenty-seven years, turning our children and grandchildren into a permanent debtor class, or what I call permanent indentured interest payers, a term that could very well apply to us now. Our standard of living is now going down, year after year. Many of the good jobs have been and now are being shipped offshore. Pension plans are being bankrupted, with some retirees now having to go back to work at minimum wage just to put food on their tables. Health care costs have soared beyond the reach of the average American and tens of millions of us have no health insurance at all. Students leave college with tens of thousands of dollars of debt, only to find that good jobs are few and far between. The list goes on and on. So, how did we get here and is there an escape route?

But, who is to blame for this? The answer is simple: We are. We average Americans have doomed ourselves. We haven't just done ourselves in; we've also consigned generations of Americans yet to come to a lower standing of living. We're the generations that defeated Nazi Germany and

Imperial Japan as well as Cold War Communism. We invented the television, the Internet, computers, rockets and technology that could take us to the moon and back, Social Security, Medicare and the greatest educational system in the world. So how did this looming disaster come about? It's simple–we bought the cure-all potion from the snake oil salesman. We've been sold a bill of goods. Remarkably, we've followed the Pied Piper.

Politicians that claim to represent us appear to be doing anything that they can to clean our clocks, to pick our pockets, to enrich themselves and their close associates beyond anyone's wildest dreams. We'll talk more about that later; however, as just one example, does it not seem strange to you that President Bush couldn't have sought out an American company to manage our ports instead of going to the United Arab Emirates, a country known to have been friendly to terrorists, to do the job? And one report states that of the 12 million illegal immigrants in this country, 1.4 million hold construction jobs. Are these jobs that Americans don't want? Construction jobs are among the best and highest paying jobs. Also, an additional $3.5 trillion in debt has been dumped on us in the past seven years by a "conservative" president and Congress, yet some of our major freeways and turnpikes are being bought up by foreign interests? What's going on here?

What is it that really matters to the average American in our everyday lives? No one can seriously argue with the fact that we need a place to sleep, a roof over our heads for ourselves and our families, steady jobs, food on our table, educations for our children, transportation to get to and from work, public safety, leisure time to enjoy the fruits of our labors and to be with our families, health care when needed, and in our old age, Social Security to ensure that we do not suffer from lack of food, clothing, shelter and health care. These are basic physical needs for all of us, regardless of race, gender or religion.

What the average American has done in the past twenty-seven years is like the head of the household who takes the family fortune to Las Vegas and blows it all at the gaming tables, leaving the family destitute. There is no honor in that. I've seen that happen to real families. There is no rational, logical, excusable reason for such conduct. It was a waste of the family's assets. It has put the family in a terrible situation. I would argue that our nation is in fact one large family. This is how Jesus viewed these things. His admonition as to our proper conduct toward one another is found at Matthew 25:40: "Whatever you do unto the least of these, you do unto me." So, just who are "the least of these?" Are they the Ted Kennedys and the Jay Rockefellers, the Paris Hiltons and the Warren Buffetts? Hardly. Those just mentioned are people who in their lifetimes will never worry about having the money to pay the utility bill, the rent, the car payment or a medical bill. They will never have to worry about losing a job, or finding a job, or going to college. Their credit card bills will always be paid—on time. The "least of these" are in fact everyday, average Americans. They are also the 30 to 40 million people in this country who go to bed hungry every night. They're the 40 to 50 million people who have no health insurance. The "least of these" include the poor who live in our inner cities with high crime rates and violence, drug abuse and despair. The "least of these" include average Americans who have been unemployed for two, three and four years in spite of their diligent search for jobs that will pay a decent wage. They are also our citizens who go off to fight wars where the apparent motive for war was nothing more than "to go to war," so that the president could have "war powers."

I've made a very strong statement above by saying that we've doomed ourselves by buying the cure-all potion from the snake oil salesman. Again, another admonition from Jesus: "Therefore by their fruits you will know them." [Matthew 7: 20] Words are cheap. Jesus warned us to beware of false prophets who come to us in sheep's clothing, but inwardly are ravenous wolves. [Matthew 7: 15] Have we average Americans been the victims of those who have come to us in sheep's clothing, claiming, for example, to be "compassionate conservatives," but who inwardly are really ravenous wolves? There is a rather simple method to find this out. One of the founders of our nation, Benjamin Franklin, is said to have a simple process by which he determined whether he should or should not do something. He would take a piece of paper and draw a line down the middle of it. He would then list all those things on the left side that favored his going forward, and on the right side of the paper he would list all those things that ruled against his going forward. At the end he would tally them up and the side with the greater number would carry the day. So, we can do that for ourselves with respect to what our government has done for the average American over the past twenty-seven years. If what the government has done has benefited us, then we should continue doing what we've been doing. If what the government has done, and is doing, has not benefited us, then we need to stop it or change the government by putting different people into office. Or, in the most extreme example, as Thomas Jefferson suggested, we change the form of government. This process is fairly straightforward. So, let's get started.

Section II:
America's National Debt

This debt perhaps should be best described as "the debt that we have dumped onto our children and our grandchildren, mere babies and the unborn." A small faction of people (politicians, industrialists, business people, and opportunists) has learned how to manipulate sincere, hard-working and God-fearing Americans in order to gain and exercise political and economic power to their benefit and to the detriment of us average Americans. This group's intent since at least 1981 has been the intentional and systematic plundering of the American treasury. For example, in 1981 when Ronald Reagan assumed the American presidency, the American national debt was less than $1 trillion ($930 billion.) Today, in 2008, only twenty-seven years later, the national debt has exploded nine fold, to $9.2 trillion. However, even this number does not represent the full extent of the onerous burden placed on the average American taxpayer. Social Security, which has run a surplus for decades, will go negative sometime between 2010 and 2015. In other words, the amount of money coming in from Social Security collections will be less than that being paid to Social Security recipients. The average American taxpayer will have to reach deeper into his pocket to make up this shortfall. Will the money be there? Will the younger generation agree to tax themselves for our profligacy? The burden does not fall on the rich. They don't pay into Social Security anyway. Money received from dividends and capital gains on the sale of stocks, businesses, real estate and the like is not liable for the payment of Social Security taxes. Instead, the burden is dumped on the average American, those who are wage earners, and those who work for their money.

In addition to having to fund the shortfall in Social Security, the American taxpayer will have to fund pension funds that have gone broke. This is the responsibility of the Pension Benefit Guaranty Corporation. PBGC is a federal corporation created by the Employee Retirement Income Security Act of 1974 (ERISA.) It currently protects the pensions of 44.1 million American workers and retirees in 30,330 private single-employer and multi-employer defined benefit pension plans. PBGC currently receives no funds from general tax revenues. Operations are currently financed by insurance premiums set by Congress and paid by sponsors of defined benefit plans, investment income, assets from pension plans trusteed by PBGC, and recoveries from the companies formerly responsible for the plans. Employers, large and small, with the help of the Bush administration and Congress, have learned how to bail out of their obligations to their pension recipients and to dump this responsibility on the PBGC. Make no mistake about it; it is only a matter of time before the average American taxpayer will also have to bail out the PBGC. Recent legislation by our representatives in Congress have stuck us average Americans with this debt, too.

However, let's take another look at the American debt and see how profoundly we've cheated ourselves and future generations by voting for the politicians who have done this to us. The United States, in 2008, is now 219 years old, its constitution having been adopted in 1789. From 1789 to 1981, the United States made the Louisiana Purchase in 1803, fought the War of 1812, fought the Mexican-American War of 1846–1848, suffered through the Civil War (1861–1865), went through several recessions, fought the Spanish-American War of 1898, the First World War, suffered through the Great Depression, built the Hoover Dam (completed in 1935) and the Tennessee Valley Authority (begun in 1933), bringing electrical power to tens of millions of Americans, fought World War II (1941–1945), rebuilt Europe through the Marshall Plan and then Japan, fought the Korean War, maintained itself throughout the Cold War, launched

NASA, sent astronauts to the moon and back, built the Interstate Highway System, fought the Vietnam War and launched the Great Society. Through all of this, the national debt in 1981 stood at less than $1 trillion (approximately $930 billion.) Please plant this number firmly in your mind.

Then, under the eight years of Ronald Reagan's presidency, the national debt ballooned to almost $3 trillion. In eight short years, we tripled our national debt. It went up another $1 trillion under the presidency of George Herbert Walker Bush, in just four years matching what it had taken almost two centuries to accumulate before that. During the eight years of the Bill Clinton presidency, the national debt climbed approximately $1.3 trillion; however, when Clinton left office the budget had not only been balanced but a surplus of approximately $500 billion had been created. The federal bureaucracy had been reduced by 50,000 and fewer people were on welfare. There was even talk of paying off the national debt in its entirety at the time that George W. Bush became president. Yes, given the trends existing at the end of the Clinton presidency, it was anticipated that America could be debt free in about ten years. Then, under the presidency of George W. Bush and a Republican-controlled congress, the national debt ballooned an additional $3.5 trillion in just six short years. Additionally, the $500 billion surplus of the Clinton administration was spent in the first six months of the G.W. Bush presidency. It simply disappeared. Where did that money go? It didn't go to Social Security or Medicare. It didn't go to build new hospitals, schools, highways or bridges. It most certainly did not go to a bunch of "welfare mothers."

So, the question is: what happened to the $8 trillion of our money that was spent in the last 27 years? Was that money spent to shore up Social Security and Medicare? Did we pay for a massive highway and bridge-building campaign? Was the money spent to build newer and better-equipped schools and hospitals? Did we use it to rebuild the inner core of our cities, helping to eliminate poverty and crime? The answer to those questions is a resounding NO. What happened was nothing less than the most massive looting of a public treasury in recorded history. And, it is not over. The Bush Administration wants to build an anti-missile defense system in the Czech Republic and Poland, thereby threatening to start a new arms race with Russia. How could this possibly benefit the average American? Why not let Western and Eastern European nations decide what kind of defense system they need? Is this simply another way for President Bush to pour billions of tax dollars into the pockets of his friends? The questions then are these: why and how did this happen? And, why does this looting continue? Why do we average Americans allow our future security to be stolen from us? Why do we permit the dumping of trillions of dollars of debt on our children and grandchildren?

Section III:
The Beginning of the End–Ronald Reagan

The beginning of the end can be placed conveniently on the shoulders of one man–Ronald Reagan. Ronald Reagan was a man with a warm, friendly exterior, but also one who believed that government was not part of today's problems, but rather that government was THE problem. In his first inaugural address given on January 20, 1981, President Reagan stated:

> But great as our tax burden is, it has not kept pace with public spending. For decades we have piled deficit upon deficit, mortgaging our future and our children's future for the temporary convenience of the present. To continue this long trend is to guarantee tremendous social, cultural, political, and economic upheavals. In this present crisis, government is not the solution to our problem; government is the problem.

In a mere eight years, President Reagan himself, absolutely going contrary to what he had said in his inaugural speech, piled deficit upon deficit, practically tripling the nation's debt, mortgaging our future and our children's future. Did he understand what he was doing? Was President Reagan a mere lackey for those with designs on plundering the U.S. Treasury? One of President Reagan's actions was to deregulate the savings and loan industry in the United States. While this may have been a good move on the face of it in order to spur competition in the industry, in fact it proved to be a disaster. What Mr. Reagan failed to do, or rather what he provided, is that the American taxpayer would foot the bill for any failed loans. This was a carte blanche for the savings and loan industry to go on a reckless and disastrous spending spree, often times making loans on properties that were more than what the properties were worth. When these loans defaulted, with the borrowers taking the money and running with it, the American taxpayer was left to pay the bill. This cost you and me, the average American taxpayer, one-half trillion dollars. Can you imagine the uproar if someone had suggested that we should give $500 billion to welfare mothers? However, there was little uproar that it went to a bunch of white men wearing white shirts and ties. Why is this?

With the Reagan presidency, we can also mark the beginning of the decline of Organized Labor in the U.S. The American middle class was built on the back of Organized Labor. The attack on Labor was brutal and direct. This occurred when Mr. Reagan fired the air traffic controllers who were striking for better wages and working conditions. In this regard, Mr. Reagan firmly established himself as an enemy of the average American citizen. The so-called conservative war against organized labor was now fully launched with the Reagan Revolution. The objective was to diminish organized labor's power in the U.S. Mr. Reagan fired the first shot with the firing of the air traffic controllers on August 5, 1981. The very next day, August 6, 1981, President Reagan began a month-long vacation at his California ranch. President Reagan banned the more than 11,000 members of the Professional Air Traffic Controllers Association from ever serving as air traffic controllers for life. Why would President Reagan act so punitively? President Clinton ended the "ban for life" but thousands were never rehired.

Ronald Reagan was born on February 6, 1911, in Tampico, Illinois. In his youth, he saw the beginnings of two industries that were in their infancy–the automobile industry and the airline industry. In his youth, there were few paved roads and virtually no airports. Few people had telephones and radios. Approximately 95% of the population lived in an agrarian setting, with the ability to have vegetable gardens, chickens, goats, cows, pigs and the like. In other words, in many respects they were self-sufficient. However, following the Great Depression and World War II, the demographics of the country had practically reversed itself–almost 95% of the population was now living in an urban setting. The American population, indeed the people of the world, had taken to the highways and airways. Large cities were beginning to spring up around the country. The American worker had become a wage earner instead of a farmer. Many people lived in large apartment complexes, without an opportunity to have their own gardens or animals.

The fact of greater interdependency among government, labor, agriculture and industry appears to have been lost on Mr. Reagan and those who supported his theory of government–that government should be starved down to a mere skeleton so that it could do little if anything for the average citizen. The stated purpose of the "Reagan Revolution" was to reduce the reliance of the American people on government. At the end of his two terms in office, Mr. Reagan viewed with satisfaction his supposed achievements. However, in fact, what Mr. Reagan had achieved was the beginning of the complete fleecing of the average American. Unlike the other major industrial nations of the world, Mr. Reagan turned the American system into a parasite that feeds on the work and energy of the average American, and in fact on a generation, or generations, not yet born. The system under Mr. Reagan, and the system under the current leadership in Washington, D.C., have and continue to exploit the average American taxpayers.

A. RONALD REAGAN AND BIG OIL

When Ronald Reagan assumed the presidency in 1981, the Department of Energy had a section involved in the study and promotion of alternative energy systems. The purpose of this section was to find various ways in which to produce energy to power our cars, provide electricity to our homes and factories, and to grow our crops. A number of new inventions were in the works and some saw fruition, such as the windmills. The income tax code provided incentives for investment in these types of projects. However, in 1984, Mr. Reagan passed down the word that the Department of Energy was not to be undertaking such studies. By 1986, the tax code was changed so that tax credits no longer went to those investing in alternative energy systems, such as the windmills. America's energy, according to Mr. Reagan and, of course, his vice-president, George Herbert Walker Bush, who was "Big Oil," was oil and gas. This action by Messrs. Reagan and Bush have cost the average American taxpayer hundreds of billions of dollars, if not trillions of dollars, in higher fuel prices and the lag in development of safer, cleaner, cheaper energy sources, such as solar, compressed natural gas and wind farms.

B. RONALD REAGAN'S THEORY OF GOVERNMENT

Ronald Reagan's theory of government can be gleaned somewhat from one of the most misattributed statements in the so-called conservative movement. In a taped speech that Mr. Reagan gave to a crowd gathered for Barry Goldwater's presidential bid in Manchester, New Hampshire, on March 5, 1964, Mr. Reagan stated:

"A democracy cannot exist as a permanent form of government. It can only exist until the voters discover they can vote themselves largess out of the public treasury."

Mr. Reagan repeated this quote on June 8, 1965, at a testimonial dinner for Rep. John M. Ashbrook in Granville, Ohio. The quote is allegedly from Alexander Tytler, an 18th century Scottish intellectual and professor. In fact, no extant writing of Tytler's contains this quote. In other words, someone else made it up. Nevertheless, so-called conservatives love to quote it.

So, what is it that Ronald Reagan really believed about this position? Was he really concerned that the masses would empty the public coffers by putting social services in place and bring an end to American democracy? Given Mr. Reagan's apparent views on government, why wouldn't he welcome such an occurrence? There is another issue concerning Ronald Reagan's view regarding government. He viewed government as "a beast." David Stockman, Ronald Reagan's budget director talked about "starving the beast," referring to the federal government. This was used supposedly as a justification to cut taxes. Without the money to support social programs, government would shrink to the point of being nothing more than a mere skeleton. Is there any rational basis for this point of view? What is the reason to cut social services? When we talk about social services are we talking about socialism? Why make such a radical departure from the rest of the industrialized world in terms of government services? Why is America so out of step with the rest of the industrialized world? Was this simply a rationale for cutting taxes on the wealthy? Was Mr. Reagan trying to protect the wealth of the rich from the so-called rampaging masses? Or, was this simply part of the plan to bring the average American worker to his knees? Why did Mr. Reagan hate the average American? Another ploy used by President Reagan and one copied by President Bush is to appoint agency heads who are nothing more than caretakers. President Reagan and President George W. Bush each took an oath that they would faithfully execute the laws of the United States. But, did they uphold this oath? There was never any intention on the part of Presidents Reagan or Bush that the agencies should actually discharge their mandated duties. One example is the Environmental Protection Agency. Another is FEMA (Federal Emergency Management Agency), for which the response (or non-response) to Hurricane Katrina's devastation is a prime example. The issue was not simply incompetence, but indifference piled on top of it.

The appointment of reactionary Supreme Court Justices to the U.S. Supreme Court (conveniently but intentionally misnamed as "conservative") by Reagan and the two Bushes is beginning to pay off for the anti-labor, big-business group. For example, in the case of *National Labor Relations Board vs. Kentucky River Community Care*, a case that began in the 1990s when a labor union sought to represent nurses and other healthcare workers at a Kentucky nursing home, the U.S. Supreme Court held that the nurses were classified as supervisors and therefore not eligible for union membership because they were a part of management. Six of the nurses at the nursing home sometimes supervised and scheduled the work of other staff. The nursing home owners argued that the nurses should therefore be excluded from union membership eligibility. Prior to President George W. Bush taking office in 2001, the NLRB had held that the nurses did not exercise sufficient independent judgment when they used their professional training to direct lesser-skilled employees in the performance of their duties. The Supreme Court, in ruling against the union, expanded the definition of "supervisor" so broadly that practically anyone might be deemed to be a part of management, and therefore ineligible for union membership. The repercussions from this court decision are already beginning to be felt in relations between employers and employees, where employees are now not being compensated time and one-half for working more than forty hours per week.

C. PLUNDERING THE NATIONAL TREASURY.

Mr. Reagan and his supporters gained a realization from the words attributed to Alexander Tytler. What they realized was that there was another way to "starve the beast," and in the process to enrich themselves beyond belief. In their minds, they could beat the masses to the public coffers. Instead of the masses plundering the treasury, a select few would do the plundering to benefit themselves only. Let the masses be damned. Their motto has been: Do it to them before they can do it to us. The only thing that they needed to do in order to ensure this was to obtain power over the government. To do this, they would have to win elections. We now witness the appearance of the political spin meisters. These are the people who know how to use propaganda to persuade a large number of people to vote against their own social and economic interests. So, what group can best be manipulated to act against its own best interests?

The plundering of the treasury has been so persistent and so extreme that those who fashion themselves as true fiscal conservatives are now taking exception to the "Bush Republicans." Former Speaker of the House of Representatives, Newt Gingrich, addressing the Conservative Political Action Committee in Washington, D.C. in early February, 2008, advised fiscal conservatives to declare their independence from the Republican Party based largely on the profligate spending patterns now promoted by Republicans. Clearly, the Republican Party no longer stands for balanced budgets or limited government intrusion into our personal lives. What we are now witnessing is nothing less than the possible, if not probable, disintegration of the Republican Party. Mr. Gingrich even advised to team up with conservative Democrats.

D. INDOCTRINATION OF THE FAITHFUL.

Some in the Republican Party decided to enlist the aid of Christians to promote their cause. These believers have become the pawns of the master manipulators. The manipulators have sowed seeds of discord, preaching hate and fear against political opponents. Through the efforts of Ralph Reed, Jerry Falwell (now deceased), James Dobson, Pat Robertson and others, many Christians have identified themselves almost exclusively with the Republican Party. However, manipulators have in many ways infiltrated and taken control of the Republican Party. A small, elite group within the Republican Party has been all too happy to let the "true believers" promote their religious causes, on the one hand, while they plunder the public treasury and cut government services, on the other hand. Included in that small elite group of manipulators are the likes of George Bush, Dick Cheney, Karl Rove and their financial supporters who are anything but "born-again Christians." It should be noted that some evangelical Christians have now had their eyes opened to the deception foisted onto them by the current Republican leadership and are moving away from the Republican Party at lightning-fast speed. Many former Republicans are now supporting a new political party called the Constitution Party.

Here's an example of how the tight knit core of opinion managers has indoctrinated the faithful. I was born and reared in Texas. In 2006, I attended a family reunion, with more than 200 present. I had this conversation with a well-educated cousin of mine who graduated from a major state-supported university in Texas. I asked my cousin what we could do about the $3.5 trillion of additional national debt run up by President Bush in the past six years. My cousin's reply was: "Don't worry about it. We'll take care of it." I then expressed grave concern about the $9 trillion that our national government is now in debt. My cousin's response was the same: "Don't worry about it. We'll take care of it." I then pointed out that Social Security would run into the red sometime between 2010 and 2015. Like a broken record, my cousin replied: "Don't worry about it. We'll take care of it." I let the matter drop at that point. Who is the "we" who is going to take care of it? My cousin is 70 years old. And how is this going to be done?

This conversation is illustrative of how the so-called conservative Republican Party operatives have misled many into believing virtually anything that is handed down as the party line. Or, it can be interpreted as simply a defensive response to a condition for which there is no reasonable or rational explanation. If taken at its face value, the response reveals a deep and profound dismissal of history and economic forces at work.

Section IV:
The Decline and Fall of Empires.

Charles A. Beard, in his excellent work, "The Economic Basis of Politics," [Alfred A. Knopf, New York, 1934], observes at page 28: "It cannot be denied that the social and economic conditions of Athens, feudal Europe, or the Stuart age were in many respects different from those prevailing in the United States. Still mankind here, as in the Old World, must struggle for existence and, allowing for the divergences in circumstances, we have no reason for assuming that the economic laws which governed in other times and other lands are without effect in this fortunate country." In other words, the economic and political forces at work on other nations are equally at work on the United States. Those same economic and political forces can also cause the United States government to collapse.

A recent example of these economic forces at work is the implosion of the Union of Soviet Socialist Republics (USSR) in 1991. The second most potent military force on earth simply collapsed in on itself. It ran out of funds. There was no longer any incentive to prop up a structure that couldn't deliver needed economic, political and social services. History is full of examples of this situation. The Ming Dynasty (1368–1644) in China collapsed and fell to the Manchus who simply rode through the northern gates and took over the Chinese empire with barely an arrow being shot in defense. This came just forty years after the famous Ming scholar, Hsü Kuang-ch'i (1562–1633) wrote one of the most controversial essays in imperial Chinese history while sitting for the *chin-shih* exam [the *chin-shih* degree was the highest degree awarded in the empire, equal, some say, to a double Ph.D. degree] at the imperial palace in Beijing in 1604. In that essay Hsü opined that one of the principal reasons for the fall of previous Chinese dynasties was the exponential growth of the imperial family. An emperor might have as many as 200 concubines in addition to his principal wife. These concubines may have as many as two, three or four children each. Many of these children would have wives, scores of concubines and even more children. All of these children and grandchildren, and on down through the generations, were princes and princesses. As such, they were entitled to support at the expense of the state. Their numbers quickly grew into the thousands and then tens and hundreds of thousands, all dependent upon the state for support. In Hsü's view, this increased burden placed on the state coffers helped to accelerate the demise of previous dynasties. The Ming Dynasty ended forty years after Hsü's essay.

A similar fate befell the Ch'ing Dynasty in China (1644–1911). It began as a robust dynasty. However, over time, it too became weak and disoriented, lacking almost completely in leadership. It is not the intent here to go into a lengthy analysis of the decline and fall of some of history's great states, such as that of Athens, the Roman Empire, the numerous Chinese dynasties, Byzantium, or even that of the Soviet Union. Suffice it to say that these governments fell principally because of internal causes and not from outside aggression. One question that arises is the issue of cause and effect. Is there an economic cause for the collapse of these states, or is there something else at work that makes the economic condition what it is prior to the collapse? The Chinese for centuries have known that there is generally a six-generation cycle to be found in Chinese families–from poverty, to comfort, to mild affluence, to affluence and then back to mild affluence, comfort and then poverty. The Soviet Union, one may argue, spent itself into oblivion by spending too much money on defense. The state's economy rotted from the inside out. By the fact that the Soviet Union had eliminated all other classes within its economy, except for the elite few Communist Party members who directed the work of the proletariat, it accelerated the process of disintegration.

Why is it that the great majority of states last no longer than two or three hundred years? Hsü Kuang-ch'i surmised that the large size and cost of supporting imperial family members put too heavy a strain on the empire's fiscal resources. One might make the same argument about the Soviet Union, except that the economic strain was caused by heavy defense spending and nothing much being spent on social services. Might not the problem be one of alienation, the alienation of the workers from the fruits of their labors? What is the function of government in this regard? When the United States was founded, one of its principal architects, James Madison, in Number Ten of the Federalist Papers, stated that the prime function of government is the protection of the different and unequal faculties of man for acquiring property. For Madison, there is no question but that politics springs from economics. [See Charles A. Beard, Ibid., pp. 29–30.] The Republican Party in 21st century America has abandoned this notion of fair play and is now engaged, at full throttle, in the subjugation of the middle-class and working-class Americans to the dominance of the wealthy.

So what happens when the wealth of a nation, the fruits of the labors of millions, is skimmed off by the few? Does there come a point in time when, without the support of the masses, the state simply crumbles? Is there a tipping point beyond which recovery is impossible? Are bankruptcy and collapse the inevitable destiny of all governments, not just the democracies as Ronald Reagan incorrectly reported that Alexander Tytler predicted? Is there a correlation between the wealth of families and the wealth of nations? Here is the fundamental factor that will cause a government to fail: when the people are weighed down by oppressive taxes, when they perceive that government is working against them and not for them, they will revolt. This revolt could be the simple act of doing nothing. What is the future that awaits our children and grandchildren? They will be paying on a debt that they had no role in creating and which gives them virtually if not absolutely no benefit. It is a pure case of taxation without representation. They will have lower-paying jobs and will be called upon to use a substantial portion of that to pay the interest on the national debt and Social Security to retired seniors, the very people who allowed the debt to accumulate in the first place. The tax payers will not find any fairness in this situation. When the government falls, how many of our precious First Ten Amendment Rights will be preserved in the new government?

Section V:
The Plundering of the Average American

A. SOCIAL SECURITY

George W. Bush made a push to "privatize" Social Security. In this he exposed himself as being a serious enemy of the average American. What kind of person would so recklessly toy with the wellbeing and welfare of millions upon millions of aged Americans? Why would a president sit by idly, watching the national debt soar $3.5 trillion in a mere six years without demanding that a large portion of that money be spent on social services such as schools, health care, job training, hospital construction, Medicare, Medicade and Social Security? What kind of person would dump trillions of dollars of debt on mere children who had no opportunity to vote on the indebtedness while giving unneeded tax breaks to Big Oil? This is obviously taxation without representation, a principal cause of the American Revolution. Is there anything moral about such conduct? And yet, a contemporary Republican supporter dismisses the matter thusly: "Don't worry about it. We'll take care of it." Well, just who is this "we." And how will it be taken care of? As Charles Beard pointed out ninety years ago in the lectures that he gave at Amherst College, the United States is not immune from the forces that have worked on governments since time immemorial. Perhaps it is a lesson that is never learned. Those who do not learn from past mistakes are doomed to repeat them. What happens to the millions of American senior citizens when the government runs out of money to pay Social Security? Will they live out their remaining days in poverty and destitution? Will millions starve to death, freeze to death, or die for lack of proper medical care?

B. WAR VERSUS DOMESTIC SPENDING

President Bush rushed American troops precipitously into a foreign invasion of a sovereign nation based on the claim that it had weapons of mass destruction and that it would most probably soon use them against the United States. In doing so, he has caused the loss of tens and even hundreds of thousands of innocent lives and the expenditure of hundreds of billions of dollars of American taxpayers' money. These hundreds of billions of dollars, some claim, are not part of the $3.5 trillion deficit run up by Mr. Bush and the Republican-controlled Congress from 2001 to 2007, but rather are yet to be accounted for. These hundreds of billions of dollars, had they been spent on domestic social matters, could have solved any alleged problem with Social Security, could have cut the cost of prescription drugs, built schools, highways, bridges, etc., creating hundreds of thousands if not millions of jobs for Americans. While spending hundreds of billions of dollars on an ill-advised and unprecedented invasion of a foreign nation, the president and Congress have cut spending on social programs for American citizens. It is reminiscent of the actions by Ronald Reagan when he became president of the United States. President Reagan cut support of programs that helped to treat and house the mentally and emotionally ill people in the U.S. Shortly after the funding was stopped, the streets in many towns across the nation were flooded with mentally and emotionally ill people wandering about, sleeping in cardboard boxes and under overpasses and bridges. These were people who had no capability of supporting themselves, for whatever reason. What kind of Christian president would do this to helpless people? Remember the one-half trillion dollars dumped into the pockets of sane, white men with the savings and loan fiasco? Why couldn't Mr. Reagan have shown as much compassion for the mentally ill? "Therefore, even as you do it unto the least of these, you do it unto me."

C. MINIMUM WAGE

Another example of exploitation of the average American by the Republican-controlled congress is the minimum wage. The minimum wage going into 2007 was $5.15 per hour, where it had been since 1997. Because of inflation, that wage was worth about $4.00 compared to 1997, a 20% decrease in purchasing power. Minimum wage workers, many of whom are seniors who are struggling to pay for prescription drugs, earn less than $11,000 annually, which is about $6,000 below the federal poverty level. By contrast, since 1997 Congress has given itself eight pay raises, amounting to a more than 20% increase. And yet, many Americans in dire financial straits keep voting for politicians that vote directly against the economic and social interests of average Americans. Frank Thomas has written about this curious phenomenon in *What's the Matter with Kansas?* Why is this allowed to happen? Are we average Americans just plain stupid? What are we trying to accomplish when we put these people into office? The good news is that in 2007 a Democratic-controlled Congress has passed legislation raising the minimum wage and President Bush has signed it, proving that whom we send to Washington does make a difference.

This is where the likes of Karl Rove come into the picture. Many people get angry when comparisons about the Bush administration have been made to Hitler. However, if one were to read that portion of *Mein Kampf* that deals with propaganda, one would find what appears to be the blue print for the machinations of Mr. Rove. Hitler saw the common people as being ignorant and easily swayed. Hitler believed that their memories were short and that important lessons were soon forgotten. Hitler had no trouble with disseminating lies in order to win public support. While Hitler did incorporate Christianity into his cause, he did take exception with one practice currently used by modern-day Republican propagandists: Hitler thought that those who hid behind religion to advance a political cause were beneath contempt. But for Karl Rove and his strategists, it is precisely the religious connection that had kept them in power. They had learned to manipulate the religious faithful. As George Bush stated in a speech given on March 31, 2001, in Washington, D.C.: "You can fool some of the people all the time, and those are the ones you want to concentrate on." Bush and Rove have done this by the use of wedge issues, such as issues involving abortion and gay marriage.

What exactly is a wedge issue? I just mentioned abortion and gay marriage. In his 2004 presidential campaign, President Bush campaigned hard, promising to push for a constitutional amendment that would "preserve the sanctity of marriage," whatever that might be given that 50% or more of heterosexual marriages in the United States end in divorce. The truth is, there is nothing about a gay relationship that adversely affects any of us. Mr. Bush also spoke about outlawing abortion. The truth is, no one will ever force you or one of your family members to get an abortion. Is a woman, in their view, nothing but a walking womb, a child-bearing machine, with no brain of her own? So what did Mr. Bush do about these two issues following his re-election? Nothing. The answer is, nothing. Many Christians feel betrayed and swindled by Mr. Bush's abandonment of these issues after the election was over. But, he did get their vote. Mr. Bush will not run for political office again. At this point Mr. Bush couldn't care less that these people feel betrayed by his inaction. Nevertheless, his conduct may have struck a serious body blow to the Republican Party.

Is George W. Bush sincere in his courting of Christian America? Does he really think of himself as a Christian and a 'born-again' follower of Jesus? Or is Bush's Christian conversion just another big lie? Was becoming a Christian something he needed to invent to achieve his political ends? In 1978 George Bush ran for Congress in Texas. He was defeated because his opponent was able to portray him as a carpet-bagging playboy from Harvard, from which Bush earned an MBA degree. It was his first and most important political lesson, and a lesson he never forgot. His opponent in that race, Congressman Kent Hance, said in retrospect that the lesson Bush learned from that campaign was that "he wasn't going to be out-Christianed or out-good-old-boyed again." And indeed he hasn't been.

D. MILITARY-INDUSTRIAL COMPLEX AND DOMESTIC SPYING

President Dwight D. Eisenhower, in his farewell address to the nation on January 17, 1961, stated, in part, the following:

> This conjunction of an immense military establishment and a large arms industry is new in the American experience. The total influence—economic, political, even spiritual—is felt in every city, every Statehouse, every office of the Federal government. We recognize the imperative need for this development. Yet we must not fail to comprehend its grave implications. Our toil, resources and livelihood are all involved; so is the very structure of our society.
>
> In the councils of government, we must guard against the acquisition of unwarranted influence, whether sought or unsought, by the military-industrial complex. The potential for the disastrous rise of misplaced power exists and will persist.
>
> We must never let the weight of this combination endanger our liberties or democratic processes. We should take nothing for granted. Only an alert and knowledgeable citizenry can compel the proper meshing of the huge industrial and military machinery of defense with our peaceful methods and goals, so that security and liberty may prosper together.

That is amazing insight. President Eisenhower's words and warnings appear to be lost on present day Americans. How could we forget this ominous warning so quickly? President Eisenhower warned us that the total influence would be economic, political and even spiritual. He warned us that this could come to endanger our liberties and our democratic processes. And, that is exactly what has happened. President Bush has been conducting secret spying campaigns against ordinary Americans almost since he took office, even before 9/11, clearly in violation of the Constitution. Mr. Bush claims that he has this authority and that this is necessary to protect us from terrorists. But, as Benjamin Franklin is reported to have said in 1759: "Those who would give up essential liberty to purchase a little temporary safety, deserve neither liberty nor safety." Why would Mr. Bush take away our essential liberties allegedly for the purpose of purchasing a little temporary safety? Why would Mr. Bush resort to illegal spying on American citizens when he could easily have obtained search warrants from the Foreign Intelligence Surveillance Act (FISA) court after the fact? The law allows the president to intercept communications and then, after that, go to court to get the court's approval of the wire tap. Arguably, unless Mr. Bush was engaged in illegal activities, there was no reason not to get proper court approval of the spying. We are reminded again of President Eisenhower's warning. Ask yourself this: Would you be comfortable with this kind of government spying if it were done at the direction of President Clinton, or any Democratic president? If not, the suggestion then is that there is something wrong with the process.

The American expenditure on the military-industrial complex equals the expenditures made by the rest of the world's nations combined. The question that one must ask is: why? Why does the United States continue to spend money on war matters instead of social programs? What nation in the world today would dare launch a strike against the United States? Its fate would be almost certain: complete annihilation. Saddam Hussein knew this. That is why it is preposterous to suppose that he would have used nuclear weapons against the United States, even if he had had them. The United States has enough nuclear weapons stockpiled literally to destroy the world, to say nothing about an individual country, including Russia. Given America's geographical location (protected by two oceans on the east and west, and bounded by friendly nations on the north and south) and its armaments, no country would dare to mount a nuclear attack on the U.S. There are some possible scenarios in which one could imagine the world ganging up on the U.S. One would be that the U.S. had become such a fascist, aggressive rogue nation, launching unprovoked, unilateral invasions of independent nation-states, that a curtailment would be necessary. And, in such an event, military action may not necessarily be the action of first resort. More than likely, economic sanctions would be imposed first. Another possible scenario would be that a rogue state, such as North Korea, could launch an attack; however, such an attack would result in the complete devastation of the government supporting such an attack. North Korea, as we know it, would be obliterated. So, why do we continue to spend all this money on military matters instead of schools, hospitals, Social Security, job creation and other things to benefit the American people? The answer is, I would submit, that our treasury has been captured by the few who continue to plunder it systematically, to the detriment of ordinary Americans. We should heed President Eisenhower's warning and do something about it.

E. MEDICARE DRUG BILL—THE TOTAL SCREWING OF THE AVERAGE AMERICAN

The Republican congress pushed the Medicare Prescription Drug, Improvement, and Modernization Act (Public Law 108–173, also called "MMA legislation") through to approval in 2003 and the bill was signed by President Bush on December 8, 2003. The bill produced the largest overhaul of Medicare in its 38-year history. One month after Mr. Bush signed the bill, the ten-year cost estimate was boosted to $534 billion, up more than $100 billion over the figure presented by the Bush administration during Congressional debate. The inaccurate figure helped secure support from fiscally conservative Republicans who had promised to vote against the bill if it cost more than $400 billion. President Bush knew that it would cost more than $400 billion but lied about it. It was reported that administration officials had concealed the higher estimate and threatened to fire government analyst Richard Foster if he revealed it. **Congress actually wrote into the bill a provision that prohibits the Federal government from using its superior purchasing power to negotiate discounts with the drug companies.** And these people are supposed to be representing us? Virtually all other industrialized nations routinely use their purchasing power to obtain cheaper prescription drugs for their citizens. This is simply yet another example of how the Bush administration and the Republican-controlled congress have exploited the average American in order to benefit the chosen few. Can we really say that these people are representing us? Why would our own representatives make it impossible for us to get life-saving drugs at a lower price?

F. BANKRUPTCY

President Bush's attack on the average American, with the help of the then Republican-controlled Congress, also finds body in the recently-enacted bankruptcy reform bill. This bill is nothing but an accelerated attack on America's most vulnerable citizens. Of course, there will always be some who take advantage of a program; however, this bill affects millions of innocent Americans. The bankruptcy bill effectively turned the Federal Government into a collection agency for greedy credit card companies and banks that make tens of billions of dollars from late charges alone. Basically what is happening is that, except for the rich, people who declare bankruptcy will not be able to get out of debt–they will continue to make payments indefinitely. Charles Dickens wrote about debt-enslavement almost two centuries ago. What are we doing? The credit card companies are making record profits. And, oh yes, Congress did manage to protect rich people from bankruptcy by allowing them to create 'asset protection trusts.'

Bankruptcy court records clearly show that more than half of the people who file for bankruptcy list unpaid medical bills as a principal debt. The United States is the only industrialized nation that does not provide all of its citizens with basic health care. And the question is: why not? In twenty-six years we've run up a debt of an additional $8 trillion. We were the richest nation in the world. Why couldn't we have at least provided our people with health care?

Travis B. Plunkett, legislative director for the Consumer Federation of America, a nonprofit research and advocacy group, said this about the bankruptcy bill: "It's not a reform bill, it's a special-interest special bill. It's a triumph of big banks and other lenders over the public interest. It's going to make it more difficult for families who have suffered genuine financial misfortune to get a fresh start in bankruptcy, and it rewards reckless and sometimes abusive practices by the credit card companies."

G. Illegal Immigration

It is estimated that there are between eleven million and thirteen million illegal immigrants (aliens) in this country, most coming from Mexico and Central America. The Bush administration claims that these people do jobs that the average American does not want to do; however, one recent report states that 1.4 million construction jobs are held by these illegal immigrants. Are those really jobs that Americans don't want? Congress has debated a bill to grant amnesty to the 11 to 13 million illegal immigrants. If such a bill passes, these people will be allowed to bring their families into the country. One respected organization has estimated that this will cause an influx of an additional 70 million people. These 70 million people will probably not be able to speak, read or write English. They will need health care and their children will need to be educated. They come from different cultures. How will the local school systems, police departments, health care services and housing handle this influx? These issues have little to do with civil rights or racism. They have everything to do with the welfare and wellbeing of the average American. No nation could or would accept such an influx, one amounting to 25% of its population. It is a recipe for disaster. These immigrants provide vital economic services in many cases and their wholesale departure could cause serious economic problems here in the U.S. Nevertheless, no viable solution appears to be on the docket in Congress or at the White House. Talk of building a fence along the U.S.-Mexican border would be laughable if it weren't so pathetic. Why aren't our representatives in Congress working on this issue? In the meantime local governments are stretched to the limits by having to fund education and health care for the immigrant families.

Section VI:
George W. Bush's duplicity.

A. GEORGE W. BUSH AND THE UNITED STATES CONSTITUTION

It has been reliably reported in *Capitol Hill Blues* on December 5, 2005, that in a meeting with Republican Congressional leaders to discuss the renewal of the Patriot act that President Bush called the Constitution "nothing but a goddamned piece of paper." Here is how it was reported:

Bush on the Constitution: 'It's just a goddamned piece of paper'
By DOUG THOMPSON
Dec 5, 2005, 07:53

Last month, Republican Congressional leaders filed into the Oval Office to meet with President George W. Bush and talk about renewing the controversial USA Patriot Act.

Several provisions of the act, passed in the shell shocked period immediately following the 9/11 terrorist attacks, caused enough anger that liberal groups like the American Civil Liberties Union had joined forces with prominent conservatives like Phyllis Schlafly and Bob Barr to oppose renewal.

GOP leaders told Bush that his hardcore push to renew the more onerous provisions of the act could further alienate conservatives still mad at the

President from his botched attempt to nominate White House Counsel Harriet Miers to the Supreme Court.

"I don't give a goddamn," Bush retorted. "I'm the President and the Commander-in-Chief. Do it my way."

"Mr. President," one aide in the meeting said. "There is a valid case that the provisions in this law undermine the Constitution."

"Stop throwing the Constitution in my face," Bush screamed back. "It's just a goddamned piece of paper!"

I've talked to three people present for the meeting that day and they all confirm that the President of the United States called the Constitution "a goddamned piece of paper."

And, to the Bush Administration, the Constitution of the United States is little more than toilet paper stained from all the shit that this group of power-mad despots have dumped on the freedoms that "goddamned piece of paper" used to guarantee.

Attorney General Alberto Gonzales, while still White House counsel, wrote that the "Constitution is an outdated document."

Imagine, if you will, George W. Bush sitting in a circle with Thomas Jefferson, Benjamin Franklin, James Madison, Alexander Hamilton, George Washington, John Adams, Patrick Henry and others, and with a smirk on his face, declaring to them: "The Constitution is nothing but a goddamned piece of paper." What hubris and condescension on the part of George W. Bush. Is this what we've come to? Are we now so degraded that we toss out eight hundred years of struggle, from the Magna Carta to the present, in a fit of ignorance, fear and self-absorption? Do we simply discard as irrelevant the millions who have fought and died in order that we might enjoy the rights and privileges contained in the Constitution of the United States?

B. National Security.

The disclosure of the identity of Valerie Plame, an undercover agent for the CIA, was a direct violation of the Intelligence Identities Protection Act of 1982 (50 U.S.C. 421 et seq.) Pertinent provisions of the Act are reproduced here:

TITLE 50—WAR AND NATIONAL DEFENSE
CHAPTER 15—NATIONAL SECURITY

SUBCHAPTER IV—PROTECTION OF CERTAIN NATIONAL
SECURITY INFORMATION

Sec. 421. Protection of identities of certain United States

undercover intelligence officers, agents, informants, and sources

(a) Disclosure of information by persons having or having had access to classified information that identifies covert agent
Whoever, having or having had authorized access to classified

information that identifies a covert agent, intentionally discloses any
information identifying such covert agent to any individual not authorized to receive classified information, knowing that the information disclosed so identifies such covert agent and that the United States is taking affirmative measures to conceal such covert agent's intelligence relationship to the United States, shall be fined

not more than $50,000 or imprisoned not more than ten years, or both.

Robert Novak has now revealed to the world that President Bush's chief advisor, Karl Rove, was one of his sources that Valerie Plame was an undercover agent for the Central Intelligence Agency. The other was former Deputy Secretary of State, Richard Armitage. Robert Novak had no authorization to receive that classified information. President Bush told us all that he would find out who disclosed that information and would then punish that person. It is now evident that Mr. Bush all along knew who leaked Valerie Plame's identity to Robert Novak and in fact probably authorized it. In other words, George Bush lied to the entire nation about this matter from the very beginning. And what has happened to Messrs. Rove and Armitage? Nothing. Mr. Bush lied when he said that he would do something about a violation of law that should put Mr. Rove and Mr. Armitage in prison. And Congress, has it brought impeachment charges against Mr. Bush? The matter hasn't even been discussed. And this following Mr. Bush's virtual pardon of Scooter Libby who was convicted of lying to the FBI about the disclosure of Plame's identity. Given Mr. Bush's actions towards Scooter Libby, what we can expect from Mr. Bush just prior to his leaving office is a wholesale pardon of his entire administration for crimes, including Vice-President Cheney, Secretary of State Condoleezza Rice, Karl Rove, and others. There will be a miscarriage of justice in his doing so.

Section VII:
The real agenda.

A. THE SELLING OF AMERICA

One sometimes wonders if Mr. Bush is more interested in representing Americans or Middle Eastern Arab potentates. For example, two days after September 11, 2001, Mr. Bush authorized just one flight in America's skies. That flight was the airplane that took the bin Laden family out of the United States back home to Saudi Arabia, the home of fifteen of the nineteen terrorists who struck on 9/11. Then, without running the matter past Congress, Mr. Bush wanted to award the management of at least six of our major ports to the United Arab Emirates, a country known to have been friendly to terrorists and even helped them with some of their banking transactions. And now, instead of using some of the $3.5 trillion in debt that Mr. Bush and his colleagues in the then Republican-controlled Congress ran up in the first six years of the Bush presidency to buy for the American citizen major turnpikes and bridges in this country, they are being sold to foreign interests instead. "By their fruits, so shall you know them."

B. CHURCH AND STATE

This issue is always a sensitive one. It is so sensitive that the Founding Fathers put this into the First Amendment to the Constitution. The First Amendment, ratified on December 15, 1791, states simply: **"Congress**

**shall make no law respecting an establishment of religion, or prohibit-
ing the free exercise thereof; or abridging the freedom of speech, or of
the press; or the right of the people peaceably to assemble, and to peti-
tion the Government for a redress of grievances."** They wanted to be
certain that the church stayed out of government, and for the protection of
the churches, that government stayed out of the churches. Yet Mr. Bush,
with his so-called faith-based initiative, has been giving billions of dollars
to Christian churches. This conduct not only violates the United States
Constitution, it is an unhealthy relationship between state and church,
analogous to a mother breast feeding her ten-year old son. Everyone
knows that such conduct is wrong. Jesus said to render unto Caesar that
which is Caesar's. The lines between church and state need to be clear. Mr.
Bush will not always be in office. What will subsequent presidents demand
of churches now that they're receiving taxpayer money? Let's not be so easily duped.

One wonders what Mr. Bush's agenda really is. For example, a Christian is often defined as one who believes that Jesus is the son of God. Some
believe that one can only achieve salvation and go to heaven by accepting
Jesus as one's Lord and Savior. Yet Mr. Bush claims that anyone who has
faith, faith in the God of the Jews, the God of the Muslims, in Hinduism,
in Buddhism, will go to heaven. This is not what a Christian believes. So,
is Mr. Bush stringing Americans along when he claims to be "born again?"
A lot of people voted for Mr. Bush because of this claim on his part. However, as we know, we know them by their fruits and deeds, not by their
words.

C. WELFARE

Few words invite attention or scorn as much as the word "welfare." So-
called conservative Republicans use it to justify tax cuts and cuts in social
welfare programs. However, there is a lie that lurks behind and beneath

their pronouncements about being against welfare. In fact, those who denounce welfare are its greatest supporters. So, just what is welfare? When a company with 10,000 acres of cotton warrants gets paid millions of dollars in subsidies, is that welfare? When large oil companies (with record-breaking profits) get billions of dollars in tax breaks, is that welfare? When Congress passes laws that allow a major corporation to dump its employee retirement plan and walk away Scot free, is that not welfare? The answer to the questions is yes because welfare is nothing more than a benefit given over to a person or entity by the government. Income tax cuts for the wealthy are a form of welfare. Non-compete contracts handed out to companies such as Halliburton and Bechtel are a form of welfare. So, when the so-called conservatives claim that they are against welfare, why then do they give it away to their large campaign contributors? When the so-called conservatives claim that they are fiscal conservatives, why then do they run up the national debt an additional $3.5 trillion in a mere six years? This is more than three and one-half times what our national debt was in the first 192 years of America's existence. Conservative? "By their fruits, so shall you know them." Recently, former speaker of the House of Representatives, Newt Gingrich, while addressing the Conservative Political Action Committee in Washington, D.C. on February 8, 2008 stated that the conservatives should distance themselves from the current Republican Party.

D. CONCEALED INTENTIONS—WHAT THE SO-CALLED CONSERVATIVES FAILED TO TELL YOU ABOUT THEIR AGENDA

Suppose the so-called conservatives had drawn up this platform, in these words, and presented it to the American people. "We are going to abolish Social Security. The best way for Americans to take care of themselves is to keep government out of their lives. We are going to abolish the public school system. Americans themselves can best decide how to educate their children. We are going to do away with any sort of national health system. People are better off when they and their doctors work things out between themselves. We are going to do away with workers' compensation laws. These matters are best when handled by the free market. We will do away with the Federal Emergency Management Agency (FEMA.) Local governments are much better positioned to handle natural disasters occurring in their own area. We will abolish the first ten amendments to the constitution. For a government to be effective in protecting its citizens from terrorists and foreign threats, the government needs to have the unfettered ability to obtain information, seize evidence, and to interrogate suspects without undue burdens being imposed upon it. Furthermore, you can forget all the talk about balancing the budget, fiscal conservatism, and full employment. Those issues have been over rated. We're going to run the national debt up to an amount that can hardly be imagined. And, we're going to promote the shipping of the really good paying jobs to foreign lands, where the work can be done much cheaper, thereby enhancing the profits of the company. We are going to change the laws to benefit the wealthy at the cost of the average American."

Suppose that they told you this in so many words? Would you still vote for those people? Well, in fact, they have told us this. We know that actions speak louder than words. Remember: "Therefore by their fruits you will know them." You know that the people you've voted for have nothing but contempt for you and me. They punish us for what they perceive to be our stupidity and gullibility. These folks are nothing but pranksters, and they think that all of this is just fun and games. However, you and I know that it is not fun and games. We have families to support. And it is our children and family members who are dying and being permanently injured in ill-conceived foreign aggressions.

E. PREACHING AND TEACHING HATE

President Bush and his campaign advisors, Karl Rove and others have learned to manipulate Republican Christians. They know that Christians hate evil, so they characterize their opponents in a very negative light. An excellent example of this is the conduct of the Swift Boat Veterans for Truth who savaged the war record of presidential candidate John Kerry during the 2004 presidential campaign. Senator John Kerry was an officer who served in the Vietnam War. He was wounded three times and was engaged in at least one fire fight, killing an enemy combatant. Kerry returned to the U.S. and engaged in opposition to the war. The chief architect of the Vietnam War, Robert S. McNamara, has since admitted that the Vietnam War was wrong and ill conceived. Mr. McNamara has apologized to the people for his part in the war, a war that claimed more than 58,000 American lives. Kerry's opponent in the presidential election, George W. Bush, by contrast, served occasionally in the Texas Air National Guard instead of going to Vietnam, being decertified from flying because he failed to appear for a physical exam, an exam that probably would have revealed the presence of drugs and alcohol in his system. George Bush has admitted to having been a user of drugs and alcohol. However, Mr. Bush's military records have since been sealed. So, while, by contrast, Kerry's service was laudable and Bush's condemnable, Kerry's record is the one that was trashed by the opposition. In talking with Bush supporters, one was surprised to find the venom that they felt toward Senator Kerry and his very accomplished wife, Teresa Heinz Kerry. How can so-called Christians be moved to hate so?

Senator Kerry did not apparently have the stomach to go for the gut instead of the head. For example, during the first presidential debate, President Bush was clearly wired (the receiver was clearly visible under his suit jacket) and was receiving input from some behind-the-scenes actor, perhaps Karl Rove. Senator Kerry and the Democrats did not seize on this opportunity to savage George Bush as a puppet. Had they done so with the vigor that the Swift Boat Veterans for Truth savaged Senator Kerry's actual war record, perhaps the election would have ended differently. Yet the Democrats are labeled as being immoral and anti-Christ. Remember, by their fruits so shall you know them. Tragically, no Democrat (except, perhaps, Howard Dean) stepped forward to expose the lies and misdeeds of the current Bush administration and the former Republican-controlled Congress.

F. The Restoration of Israel

Many people support those who claim to be Christian Republican politicians because of their belief in the second coming of Jesus Christ. Some believe that there will be a Millennium and that this will occur with the second coming of Jesus. They also believe that before the Millennium can begin, Israel must be restored to Palestine. Therefore, in order to accelerate the second coming of Jesus, fundamentalist Christians are ardent supporters of Israel, believing that the second coming will occur when the Jews are restored to Palestine. This in part helps to explain their support of a merger of Christianity and the U.S. Government. The Jews retaking Palestine helps to ensure the early arrival of Jesus. George Bush has seized upon the beliefs of these people and has increased the financial support of Christian churches by the federal government. Some say that George Bush's Christianity merely provides a convenient explanation for his transformation from a youthful degenerate to a redeemed politician. Mr. Bush's professed Christianity has earned him the loyal following of many Christians. But, that support is beginning to wane as more and more people look to what Mr. Bush does, instead of what he says.

Conclusion

The founding fathers were mindful that differences in the accumulation of property, or wealth, would divide people into different factions and different political parties. This, they knew, had been true since ancient times. The task at hand was how to put together a government that could meet the needs of all the people. This was in part the reason why the House of Representatives was based on population, while the Senate was based on property, without regard to population. The concern that the founders had was that unchecked power would lead to the dispossession by one group of the property of the other. And, today, we see that activity at work.

Now, back to Ben Franklin. Have you made your own list? Have you put down on one side of the paper all the ways in which government has made things better for you in the past 27 years, and on the other side all the things that government has done that has made it worse for you? Do this. And, also, do this for the politicians who represent you, starting with President Bush, your U.S. Senators, your Congressman, and so on. It is time to give each and everyone of them a report card. Pay no attention to which political party they belong to. Contrary to what some may claim or want you to believe, God hasn't chosen any political party over the other. Some folks might want you to think otherwise, but you know that that is not the case. No one doubts President Jimmy Carter's Christian faith and he is a full-fledged Democrat. Ralph Nader, a Christian, ran as a presidential candidate for the Green Party in 2000. I'm sorry to say that in my own list on President Bush and the Republican-controlled Congress, I found not one positive. They were all negative, starting with the invasion of Iraq based on admittedly false information, running up a further deficit of $3.5

trillion in just six years, trying to kill Social Security, passing an unconscionable Medicare Drug Prescription bill, making bankruptcy virtually impossible (shades of debtor's prisons from two centuries ago), the Katrina debacle, domestic spying, torture of prisoners, and on and on. I'm sorry that this is how this turned out. I wish that it could have been otherwise, but letting the wish father the thought has never done anyone any good. We really do need to deal simply, fairly and directly with the brutal facts.

We all know that education is the key to a healthy democracy. We let some things slip by in recent years. We haven't been on our toes. Do we blame this as the effect of television? Do we simply listen and believe everything told to us by the politicians? When, if ever, will we rise up and take what is rightfully ours? Why do we let our political leaders squander our taxes? Will we continue to allow our work and production to be stolen from us and plundered by the few who pretend to be working for us? Simply put, government is not a "beast." No one has found a system in the past eight thousand years to take the place of government. For sure, government is not perfect. But nothing has been found to take its place. Politics is, after all, about the possible, not the perfect. Compromise is inevitable in any democratic process. Ideologues are, at heart, anti-democratic.

Jesus said that we should render unto Caesar that which is Caesar's. Jesus never said that that government is best that governs least. Life, economy and society in the twenty-first century are complicated. Government is a useful tool that can help us to help ourselves and each other. It is a tool that can also be misused, as we are now witnessing and as we have seen throughout the long course of history. The sooner we reject the superficial lies of the so-called conservatives (as Newt Gingrich has), the sooner we'll be able to get back on track, assuming that it is not now already too late for the government known as the United States of America. For the time being we are all little Nero's, fiddling away while Rome burns. History, most likely, will record us as the generation that failed democracy, that failed America.

978-0-595-41028-6
0-595-41028-6

www.ingramcontent.com/pod-product-compliance
Lightning Source LLC
Chambersburg PA
CBHW050341290526
45785CB00006B/2580